PRAISE FOR SANKI SAITŌ

"An important poet deserving of this new exhaustive translation, made eminently more accessible by Masaya Saito's painstaking biography. Often his own worst enemy, Sanki's haiku plumb the depths of a turbulent, iconoclastic life during Japan's embrace of modernity and war."
—Paul Miller, editor, *Modern Haiku*

"At a time when English-language haiku is exploring new directions in form and content, these fresh translations of Sanki's haiku remind us that the seasons and their manifestations are, as he puts it, 'nothing but the outermost layer of the truth of actual existence,' and that it is the purpose of all haiku 'to immerse ourselves deep in the truth of actual being.'"
—Lee Gurga, editor, *Modern Haiku Press*.

OTHER BOOKS BY SANKI SAITŌ
IN ENGLISH TRANSLATION

Selected Haiku 1933-1962
The Kobe Hotel: Memoirs

"THREE DEMONS": A STUDY ON SANKI SAITŌ'S HAIKU

Sanki Saitō (1900-1962)
&
Ryan Choi

OPEN LETTER
LITERARY TRANSLATIONS FROM THE UNIVERSITY OF ROCHESTER

ISBN (pb): 978-1-960385-27-7
ISBN (ebook): 978-1-960385-28-4

This project is made possible by the New York State Council on the Arts with the support of the Office of the Governor and the New York State Legislature.

NEW YORK STATE OF OPPORTUNITY. | Council on the Arts

Grateful acknowledgment is made to the following publications, where sections of this book have appeared, sometimes in different form:

Cincinnati Review, Denver Quarterly, Harvard Review, Kenyon Review, New American Writing, Ninth Letter, Poetry Northwest, Poets.org, The Spectacle, TriQuarterly, and *The White Review.*

Cover design by Nicholas Motte

Published by Open Letter at the University of Rochester
Morey 303, Rochester, NY 14627
www.openletterbooks.org

Printed on permanent/durable acid-free paper in the United States.

"THREE DEMONS": A STUDY ON SANKI SAITŌ'S HAIKU

For Christopher, Dylan, and Elias.

I

*Machine
guns
between their brows—*

blood flowers bloom.

Child of summer
dawn—

tracing
horses in the mud.

Midnight

Skylarks

under storm, ferry

themselves one
by one.

Rage

Volcanic
ash-
sprinkled highlands:

jittery dance
of
the jewel beetles.

Sunflower

petals,
pattering on

a black mass
of
ants.

Money

Flesh-
colored spring

     moon,
     flaring
above the graves.

     Hitched

to the North Star, the
pillar of ice grows fat.

Airstrip, yellowing—

     terminal
in the winter

sea.

Cold seas

Pilot and dog
     frolic
through dead grass

fields
     and
roll around.

Right eye

Winter sea

     Angry
about money,
     sweat

     drips
on dirt.

Pools

Giant lilies

     in
     the air
conditioning.

Ponytails

Girls college—

     lamps lit, the
     ancient crows.

Pilot and

A tipsy
man starts

to cry
in his mildew-ridden

home.

Meadow

Dead
horses

     in mud blow
up
with mud.

Graduation day—

ponytails, inlaid
with
     drops of snow.

Dawn

Tracing

The elders' waltz, on

    the dark stone

    dew-covered stage.

    Cannon fire—
    animals and sea-

food all go cold,
shrouded in

    a haze.

Moor in ruins—

I lift the pieces
of my sister's grave
up
    into the light.

Pine cone

A district underground—

    a magician
wiggles his fingers.

Sliver

Flag
of the German Academy—

    snow-
flecked, rippling
in
the breeze.

Machine

Women on trains
depart at
the arrival

of
the lunar eclipse.

Black mass

Fair weather

morning—
        boys

peer at
the distant
castle.

Left eye

Early afternoon—

under a cascade
            of pine
cones, I buy
        a black

        mourning band.

Rooftop

Bonfires we
stoke, pierce

the
morning

        sun and
        shadows
        we stoke.

Rooftop—

doctor flapping
     his arms in
     the
     cold.

Moor in ruins

Through
     parched

meadows a father

     mumbling drunk

zigzags
home.

Mourning

As the train
     crosses into

snow lands, the
riders do not

     speak.

In mud

Left

     At midnight,

crickets

in the cold
twitching on the

     cliff.

Castle

On the muddy
stream
bank, weary

hands rise
to swat mosquitoes.

Muddy

Chauffeurs
on the street

below; tango
party above.

Morning

Grapes

Sunflowers

snapped,
uprooted,
flung to earth

by the typhoon.

Blood

Flowers bloom

Clusters of faces,
sprays

of
garlicky spit.

Sweet grapes—

      my muted rage

      at the death

of a friend.

      Jewel beetle

      Nightfall
      over lake,

match flame in
      my
whitened palm.

      Boy soldier

Graduation day—

      a gun
shell embedded
in
      his chest.

      Muted

      Shovels
in the coal piles—death

      of a maiden.

      Horn

Late
night hunger pangs,

      horns blare
in
the pit of the fog.

On the

Water pillow
gurgling, the

cold seas.

North Star

Dog-fleas that leap,
burrow into the
cold
sand dunes.

Right eye: the great river.
Left eye: the cavalry.

Lily

Autumn's
close—ocean

casting
fat fish bones.

Sunflowers

Fresh
from
overtime—

girls
in line, candied

in moon
beams.

Noble

Eyes
around the pyre,

pillar of fire

soars toward the stars.

Tipsy

Crabs skittering
about—

I squint

as
the rainbow

fades.

Petals

Light of spring—
sap

puddles
on the earth

beneath.

Line

Rooftop—

lightning

glitters on
the flesh

of noble ladies.

Wheel

Foot of the dead volcano,

lullaby voice
        of the
        wellspring.

Flesh

In summer—
        a boy paints

fishes only,

        shedding weight.

Bone

        In winter
skies above the

sea airplane
wheels stop

        spinning.

Eyes

Butterfly stirs—

        fluttering through
the first

sliver of dawn.

One boy soldier carried

        off, another
left at the gun.

II

Day of surrender—with   *dogs, I drink*   *water in despair.*

Chimney   smoke, wild dance   of virgin snow.

Green till   when: tight-   knit rice beds.

Airport—   halls of glass; clustering   hands.

House Cleansing Rites—   family cupped in   a sunny nook.

Storm   clouds; below—   hero scarecrows.

Midnight—soil, in   cold blood, mushrooms   bloom.

She: wrestling   nude with a giant   dollar bill.

Patients, up from   bed, polish the   snow-stained pane.

See little   fish, the little-   brain chills.

He: who runs   marathons about   the snow-capped peaks.

Charred   butterflies on stone,   born on a hill of stone.

Happy Birthday—faces   again in the town   square mirror.

Frosty grass, in-   rooted moon; dogs—   who squall for whom?

Night sky: twinkles of grief   at the Nativity.

In waterlogged shoes—   *farewell*   to the mildewed home.

No traces   of yesterday's snowy   fields.

Ailing palms reach   from windows, gather the   light of spring.

Rice pounded;   father's snores   rumble the home.

Old age—masks   dancing in a starlit   woods.

"Forever"   you wait, astraddle   the sunbaked stone.

Living fingers pick   green grapes; the fingers   of the dead.

I loathe them—girls   who chat with   cats in heat.

Sand   mixed atomic dust   billows—fountains, spring.

Labor Day—horses   with men knee-   deep in the paddy.

Healing Buddha Shrine—tailless   lizard licking trough   water.

Dreaming   face; *shrike-siege*—her   morning's just beginning.

I crawl through mud   trenches; *insects   crawl on me.*

Gifts for the goddess—   wet soles in   rubber boots.

Pasture: spinning   top spins back   to my palm.

Day sky above,   face of the toppled   scarecrow.

Storm clouds   birthed as eggs,   *swallowed whole.*

Dashing   up charred   hills; towers in sight.

She eats   rice cakes, goes   outdoors: legs sink into snow.

Tree   shade—suddenly, laughter   from three old ladies.

III

Snow; falls—

"... what   the snow

hath   wrought ..."
               Christmas—
               time, in the pink

of a black   man's palm.
               Cake
               in

our bellies,   beneath the

moon in   the mackerel

               sky.
               Clear winter—
               airport

at noon,   travelers

filing   through.
               Looking glass: a boy's
               glass ears, as

he munches
on plums

with   friends.
               Man
               crumples,

vomits   on the moon-

lit   steppe, and sleeps.

Reflections in
the twilight,

dingy   lake: the

shore—a   festival

of stars.
Brisk,
spring

sunrise: sweat—we
shatter

salt   crystals with

picks.
Last
night with

the boys,   peeking

into   bamboo woods.
Downpour—
skylarks,

shivering   as one,

ascend.

Tilting
castle,

ramshackle: the coldness

of the mud.
Sick
of spring,
sick of:
seeing   pine roots.

Stars in
the rain—

her telegram   reads,

"FORGIVE   ME."

On the
plateau,

my shadow   fringed with

sunflower   shadows.
Summer (of
this life)—

nightingales,

volcanic-   ash-cape

swathes   the earth.
". . . holed up
with a fever,"

delirium   flies fucking

midair.

In a mosquito
net—

blue: boy; a drawing

of   fish
Summer school—
in

hiding, he   cries

frustrated
with   arithmetic.

Hiroshima (8/6).
"Day of
Mourning"—

sand-crusted

lifebuoys.

On
beach slopes

sun   lights on

mushroom   archipelagos.
AUTUMN RAIN—
crabs

scrabbling   along the sea-

bed: haven.

Mobs—wordless,
daylong

bustle till   sunset.
Faces under
the sky:

chestnuts   green

against   the black.
Autumn—
plowing

the fields,   you dig

up your   own shadow.

*At the Lakeshore
Pavilion*—

her hairpins   *fall as*

lightning   *strikes.*

IV

Piano
plays your

sacred
winter

trees and days—

Tears— rain

on young parents' graves.

End of waltz— gourds outdoors—

outshine the mildew-
ridden home—

Sick of spring, even

sicker of jet- black tadpoles—

On
the beach slope—

sun-

burnt

mushroom

archipelago—

Town—the deepest
              winter

days,   bundles

of
        fists   on the move—

Falling silent—   a crowd

        scrambles   toward the sunset—

        Silence—   elevators climb

                through   the night,
                lightning   streaks—

                                Summer—   *daydream:*
                                            warships

                                        bob
                                        in the orphan's

                                gaze.

From   sky to earth—

        rose   petals drift   through drought—

Feast

        of rice balls: rotted   twigs, wedged

        in the hat   rack—

Lucid—
        moonrise,

        hatching

        locust eggs—

Violet—twin
     gales,

        rumpling   the boat-
                   pond skin.

Cooped in

     a white   mosquito

net,
fatigue   dense

    as iron   bricks—

      Sucking on

      pine pollen, the

         teacher
         cracks walnuts—

      Morning frost—we

         soar

      above   clouds: snow

         flits

      beneath—

Mirror cakes—
sitting,

  broken in the dark—

  Wild geese winging

    north, hauling
    commodious sacks—

      Winter—

        ambling
        cows bore

        into the dirt

        on

       the icy path—

       Machine
       guns between their brows—

       blood

      flowers bloom.

Sense of relief:

    pure salt

    crystals on soybeans—

Sun wanes: the dead

    goldfish

    plop into the bowl—

Table—
in the pine

grove, an
omelette

for my solitude—

Soldiers—

zipping by on   pitch-   black trains.

Spring—playtime:

grinding toy

trolleys
against   the hillside—

Skylarks—

in the down-
pour deliver

themselves   one

by one—

Chickens

in the spring, stagger
through the

windstorm—

Voices—in

the iron fort,
lure the buzzing

mosquitoes in—

Afraid—of red

mushrooms   that are unafraid

of me—

After   thunder, after

rain—   wooden

clogs clatter   in search of stars—

Vashikov—the Russian

growls,
swipes at   dangling

pomegranates—

Autumn harvest—

in the dirt,
you dig   up your

own   shadows—

Winter garden—
    index

finger   nicked: a girl

bleeds—

Airport—MPs

on patrol,

our   bitter farewell.

V

Sand   mixed

atomic
dust   billows—

fountain, spring.

               FORGOTTEN—
beetle,

skittering
        on a leash.

        Around
                the grave—

        virility   in
        an   ant
        swarm.

As   I leave the lake,

duck   eggs
              weep
in my   palm.

        Clouds—

sunflowers
scatter   in quest
              of
        a sun.

        Bronze Statue,   *GAZE—*

red   horizon,
        red   lightning.

GOLDFISH

lick   the underside

of an icebound   lake and
vanish   into

    the depths.

    Frosted lamps:

    SEQUENCE—

A Country Destroyed.

Foreign
    capital—
    autumn

        sunset; a piano
    sonata   plays.

    Rice gruel; in

    cats,   no such
thing   as emptiness.

Night sky,

    flower
    patch,

blackbirds taking
    flight.

    Parted lips—

frothy
plumes;   tapping

on   iron plates.

Snow   clinging
    to   window

panes, the
        faces   of disease.

FATHER   and
        SON
        plow   the autumn

fields—   one

        a mirror
        of
        the next.

        Snowed-in village:

blood   drips from

big and   tiny
                fish.

        CLOUDY—

cherry
blossoms; lonely tongue

        reflected
in   a mirror.

Maiden's   sun-

bathed grave
        blistering   to the touch.

            POWs
        asleep   on the
        rugged
        lake   shore.

MILKY WAY—

I   in whom

         the
dogs   have faith.

         Daylight
         crescent moon; and

the   lizards

         do not
somersault.

Same sun as   yesterday

                 drying sweet
         potatoes
         today.

Hands peel
      persimmons,

as my   mother

                 peeled
                 persimmons.

         Paper
cherry
blossoms, a

black man's blues
         floating

                 to the dirt.

         How not to see—

         the
shadow the cricket tows.

In   trenches,
          the divine
dog
tags   gleam.

SPRING

night—
children blink
on passing
          trains.

In the high   windows:

      no
      faces,

      only   the crimson
sun.

      This   morning, my
                    friend
      died,   and a stray

dog
      chewed on grass.

      Lofty   winter
      tunnel   encloses

the old man's gaze.

      A-Bomb   *Day,*

      loud- *speakers*

             face
      the   *open*

      sea.

VI

In the
emperor's
window, carp
streamers
swim on

strings.

Spring, cold
front—
I drum
on
the stone
castle

walls.

Rain—blessings
I
receive, I
give
to the

skylarks.

End of
day—
instead of
smiling,
we peel

grapes.

Darkness. Dogs
biting
each other
beneath
the cherry

tree.

Hiroshima—where
mouths
open for
boiled

eggs only.

Fluttering at
my
window—who
else
but the
dewspecked

birds?

Cliff's edge—
windstruck
faces of
men
and women

abreast.

Peasants huddled
under
eaves, pulled
corn
as firm
as

stones.

Rain or
shine,
money weighs
on
the town's

spine.

Monks on
deck,
the black
warships
set sail
into

the silence.

Alone, under
the
boiling sun,
a
child races
among

the tombs.

Cows, mooing
from
their bellies
at
the high
summer

surf.

Affixed to
an
evening cloud,
a
spider walks
at

peace.

Digging below
the
rainbow's rings,
our
bodies growing
wet

and wetter.

In the
ruins
of the
garden,
life collects—
sunflowers

remain.

Red spider
lilies,
seen
through
her gauze
eye

bandages.

Heart's lament—
cross-legged
I sit,
sucking
on persimmon

bits.

Black triangular
Mt. Fuji in
the summer
rain—
"Will my older

brother live?"

Mid-life. Last
summer
night—what
tired

soliloquies!

Sunset. At
last, pushed
by shoulders
the freight
car
starts to

roll.

Moon. Dog—
I
sit, stroking
its

arthritic torso.

Labor Day—
horses
and men
mired
in the
muddy

rice paddy.

Plateau. Butterflies—
gust
from below,
grass
on the

nose.

Leaves fall
on
the stray
dog,
jerking it
to

its paws.

Horns lowered,
cows
slog through
the
sheer north

winds.

Airplanes roar
above
the plots
of

frostbitten roses.

Under the
cliff,
numb from
cold,
I hammer
nails
into our

home.

Black river
fork,
jammed with
soggy
clumps of

snow.

Snow falling
on
mountain snow,
age
of my
companion's

aging wife.

In concrete
encased
in ice,
doctors
race against

time.

Cold night
breaks—
fake red
flowers
return to

view.

VII

Under the green

    persimmons,

      we

      speak

      of sad

and haunting things.

    White crescent,

mounting the

black

    of   the moon—

    will   winter

ever end?

    Raven trio—

    sing please   for

the man

    who simmers

butterburs.

    Sparrows bunked

in   the five-story

    pagoda

    flock   to

the

rice field.

    RAINBOW

anchored

    in   the dirt—

    laborers

corralled within.

    Mona Lisa

    lives in

    glass,

winter continuity.

    No sleep for

    the fish in the

far-off

    seas.

    Autumn—

    rows of breasts

    bounce along

    the   patchwork

NATIONAL

    HIGHWAY.

    Barley

reaped,

    laid to dry

on glinting stones   on

of rice.

faced with

many miseries.

the   mountain

I

Me and   the bulls

descend.

outdoors,

Summer

evenings, the

Full moon—

our tacit accord   to

stoker   strides

Banging on

through

the tin hut   like a

brave the hail-

fire-colored

storm.

railcars.

drum.

Dominion—of

Girls on the farm—

Cows at

after

the   clock's

sunset.

autumn,   thighs still

second hand; banks

Bodies gasping.

in   recovery.

of the

Boy naps,

frozen

firefly beaming

Nights   of

swamp.

cribbed in

Ignis Fatuus

his   palm.

end   on   rimy

Red plum

forest

SPECTACLE:

stalks

I escape,

a woman's hands

splitting   the   self,

                        engulfed in   deathly   playing

brittle mirror cakes.   heat.   cello.

        On razed   hills,   Shrikes'   trills   Kill the

hungry,   slice   through   the   lights.

            I fondle   Our bodies

            fired   tofu   we   cut

artillery   into   cubes.   dipped in

        shells.   autumn evening.

                                        I lay   the

            Thunder   bamboo   *MOUNTAIN PATH—*

            rending   saw to   rest   mandarin

onyx   at

            clouds, the   the gates of   oranges

                        Tōshōdai-ji.   drop

women   of   from above,

                                Sowing

            the night.   chrysanthemum   battering our

                                seeds;   paper

Shadows of   parasols.

            the   sipping

                                water;   Heat   spreads

through   as we leave   the

    the dune, as   On   the   dark   grounds of   the

                               road   Great Buddha

through   the   home,

    bottomless   lotus   statue.

      ocean.   petals

                          quivering   Moon-

Primed to   scream—   in   the   glow strokes

             TREETOP: gaze.

shrikes,   the old dog   and his

         EARTH: I stand   with our   knobby bones.

man.   starving

                                        Roosters   on

Blue—   crows   nation,   at   tiptoe—

    moping through   the   base of

                    the winter

the   drought.   rainbow.   at the clouds at

    Nut—   Warmth from   sundown.

pushed into soil, by   the   cherry

                                        On   pretty, cold

the heel   of   a   blossom   nights—I tease

boy's monstrous shoe.   trees,   the   light

          from   the   *ARC*

     shadows.   mildew-ridden home.

                    of the railroad

Farming   sweet   tracks: *MALE*   and

potatoes near   snowfall   *FEMALE*,

     a family farming   vaulting over

                              curling

     sweet   sideways.   moonlit

     potatoes.   puddles.

                    Step

     Winter—   by   step, the   Birthday. Dawn—

                    cows   press   lightning

construction men   cracks evenly

          clamber   through the   above all

          up   the   brute   north   heads.

          telegraph   winds.   Crimson, sound of the

poles and   slide

                    Shining   sacred lotus petals

     back   down.   needle   on their daily

                    quilting through   trip   to

Slow

                    the   earth.

BOY'S DAY—
nap
for the swelling
ranks of   the
Imperial Family.

Landing-
gear   wheels

whirl
above winter
mountaintops.

Spring afternoon—
on the one
red horse,
on the one   carousel.

Far edge of
the   withered

pasture,

with a sugar cube
between   her
teeth.

On   the rooftop—
no grass
or trees,

only   the   sick
and   the butterflies.

Spring—   clouds

cuddled atop the
looming
telegraph
poles.

Old man

with his wooden
flute,
under the
cool   blue

crescent moon.

Harvest Moon by
the sea—
youthful hands
dance
to the beat
of the tempestuous
waves.

Late summer—
haggard crows;

they nod and
shriek, and

nod   and shriek.

VIII

Bunched on the sod,

Slowly but surely the

clouds
and wheat stalks

stretch their bodies

POWs

Green plums,

babies crying
in

the dark

hug their knees

Only the fallen

emerald green

persimmons:

no lamps

A shepherd

lifts his staff,

to chop clouds

above the arid

meadow

Below

spring-

Winter mountain

finely
carved, trampled
by

a rainbow

lightning forks—a   queue of ice

blocks

form

Starry,
muggy

rain
front—

a
telegram

Between eye-

brows
and eyes: snowfall
and

reads:

clouds

"Forgive me"

Bury your comrade-in-arms,

shoot a pistol at the gods

ORIGINAL TEXTS

VOLUME KEY

旗 (1940) – *Flags*
三鬼百句 (1948) – *One Hundred Haiku*
夜の桃 (1948) - *Night Peaches*
今日 (1952) - *Today*
変身 (1962) – *Transformations*

—

機関銃眉間ニ殺ス花ガ咲ク (旗)

夏暁の子供よ土に馬を描き (旗)

石炭にシャベル突つ立つ少女の死 (変身)

体内に機銃弾あり卒業す (今日)

火山灰高地玉虫きりきり舞 (変身)

肉色の春月燃ゆる墓の上 (変身)

雨の雲雀次ぎ次ぎわれを受渡す (今日)

右の眼に大河左の眼に騎兵 (旗)

滑走路黄なり冬海につきあたり (旗)

断層の夜明けを蝶が這ひのぼる (夜の桃)

操縦士犬と枯草駆けまろぶ (旗)

金銭に怒れる汗を土に垂る (旗)

黴の家泥酔漢が泣き出だす (今日)

砲音に鳥獣魚介冷え曇る (旗)

汽車と女ゆきて月蝕はじまりぬ (旗)

手品師の指いきいきと地下の街 (旗)

露暗き石の舞台に老の舞 (夜の桃)

朝日さす焚火を育て影を育て (変身)

青き朝少年とほき城をみる (旗)

夏痩せて少年魚をのみゑがく (旗)

垂れ髪に雪をちりばめ卒業す (今日)

姉の墓枯野明りに抱き起す (今日)

喪章買ふ松の花散るひるさがり (旗)

顔つめたしにんにくの香の唾を吐き (旗)

雪よごれ独逸学園の旗吹かれ (旗)

酔ひてぐらぐら枯野の道を父帰る (今日)

誰も見る焚火火柱直立つを (今日)

汽車全く雪原に入り人黙る (今日)

北海の星につながり氷柱太る (変身)

向日葵を降り来て蟻の黒さ増す (今日)

きりぎりす夜中の崖のさむけ立つ (今日)

屋上に双手はばたき医師寒し (今日)

濁流や重き手を上げ藪蚊打つ (今日)

運転手地に群れタンゴ上階に (旗)

葡萄あまししづかに友の死をいかる (旗)

夜の湖あゝ白い手に燐寸の火 (旗)

腹へりぬ深夜の喇叭霧の奥に (旗)

台風が折りし向日葵伐り倒す (今日)

女学院燈ともり古き鴉達 (旗)

犬の蚤寒き砂丘に跳び出せり (今日)

秋の暮大魚の骨を海が引く (変身)

月下匂う残業終えし少女の列 (変身)

屋上の高き女体に雷光る (旗)

垂直降下青楼の午後花朱き (旗)

春の昼樹液したたり地を濡らす (今日)

死火山麓泉の声の子守唄 (変身)

蟹と居て宙に切れたる虹仰ぐ (今日)

泥濘の死馬泥濘と噴きあがる (旗)

巨き百合なり冷房の中心に (旗)

水枕ガバリと寒い海がある (旗)

機の車輪冬海の天に廻り止む (旗)

少年兵抱キ去ラレ機銃機ニ残ル (旗)

死の灰や砂噴き上げて春の泉 (変身)

湖を去る家鴨の卵手に嘆き (旗)

甲虫縛され忘れられてあり (夜の桃)

墓の前強き蟻ゐて奔走す (夜の桃)

向日葵播き雲の上なる日を探す (変身)

銅像は地平に赤き雷をみる (旗)

薄氷の裏を舐めては金魚沈む (変身)

寒燈の一つ一つよ国敗れ (夜の桃)

銀河の下犬に信頼されて行く (変身)

桜くもり鏡に写す孤独の舌 (夜の桃)

秋の暮遠きところにピアノ弾く (夜の桃)

雑炊や猫に孤独といふものなし (夜の桃)

花園の夜空に黒き鳥翔ける (旗)

昼三日月蜥蜴もんどり打つて無し (夜の桃)

白息を交互に吐きて鉄板打つ (変身)

病む顔の前の硝子に雪張りつく (変身)

父と子の形同じく秋耕す (今日)

雪の町魚の大小血を垂るる (夜の桃)

炎天の少女の墓石手に熱く (夜の桃)

青き湖畔捕虜凸凹と地に眠る (旗)

干甘藷に昨日の日輪今日も出づ (夜の桃)

柿むく手母のごとくに柿をむく (夜の桃)

紙の桜黒人悲歌は地に沈む (変身)

蟋蟀のひきずる影を見まじとす (夜の桃)

塹壕に尊き認識票光る (旗)

春の夜の暗黒列車子がまたたく (夜の桃)

男の顔なり炎天の遠い窓 (変身)

友はけさ死せり野良犬草を噛む (旗)

大寒のトンネル老の眼をつむる (夜の桃)

原爆の日の拡声器沖へ向く (変身)

限りなく降る雪何をもたらすや (夜の桃)

黒人の掌の桃色にクリスマス (夜の桃)

菓子を食う月照るいわし雲の下 (変身)

空港の青き冬日に人あゆむ (旗)

梅を噛む少年の耳透きとほる (旗)

月光の枯野を前に嘔き尽す (変身)

暗き湖のわれらに岸は星祭り (旗)

花冷えの朝や岩塩すりつぶす (夜の桃)

竹林を童子と覗く春夕べ (夜の桃)

雨の中雲雀ぶるぶる昇天す (今日)

泥濘のつめたさ春の城ゆがむ (変身)

春を病み松の根つ子も見あきたり (変身以後)

電報の文字は「ユルセヨ」梅雨の星 (変身)

高原の向日葵の影われらの影 (旗)

今生の夏うぐいすや火山灰地 (変身)

熱ひそかなり空中に蝿つるむ (旗)

青蚊帳に少年と魚の絵と青き (旗)

算術の少年しのび泣ける夏 (旗)

広島の忌や浮袋砂まぶれ (変身)

海坂に日照るやここに孤絶の茸 (今日)

秋雨の水の底なり蟹あゆむ (今日)

夕焼へ群集だまり走り出す (夜の桃)

仰ぐ顔暗し青栗宙にある (旗)

秋耕のおのれの影を掘起す (夜の桃)

湖畔亭にヘヤピンこぼれ雷匂ふ (旗)

敗戦日の水飲む犬よવれも飲む (今日)

煙突の煙あたらし乱舞の雪 (今日)

苗代の密なる緑いつまでぞ (変身)

空港の硝子の部屋につめたき手 (旗)

家中を浄む西日の隅にいる (変身)

雲厚し自信を持ちて案山子立つ (今日)

血が冷ゆる夜の土から茸生え (旗)

金銭の一片と裸婦ころがれる (旗)

病者起ち冬が汚せる硝子拭く (今日)

小脳をひやし小さき魚をみる (旗)

雪嶺やマラソン選手一人走る (今日)

岩山に生れて岩の蝶黒し (今日)

誕生日街の鏡のわが眉目 (旗)

草枯るる真夜中何を呼ぶ犬ぞ (変身)

満天に不幸きらめく降誕祭 (変身)

黴の家去るや濡れたる靴をはき (今日)

あとかたもなし雪白の田の昨日 (変身)

病者の手窓より出でて春日受く (今日)

餅搗きし父の鼾声家に満つ (今日)

老年や月下の森に面の舞 (夜の桃)

炎天の岩にまたがり待ちに待つ (変身)

青葡萄つまむわが指と死者の指 (今日)

恋猫と語る女は憎むべし (夜の桃)

死の灰や砂噴き上げて春の泉 (変身)

馬と人泥田に挿さり労働祭 (変身)

薬師寺の尻切れとかげ水飲むよ (変身)

百舌に顔切られて今日が始るか (夜の桃)

塹壕を這ふ昆虫を手にのせる (旗)

天女の前ゴム長靴にほとびし足 (変身)

枯野の中独楽宙とんで掌に戻る (変身)

倒れたる案山子の顔の上に天 (夜の桃)

雷の雲生まれし卵直ぐ呑まれ (今日)

塔に眼を定めて黒き焼野ゆく (今日)

餅を食ひ出でて深雪に脚を挿す (今日)

機関銃眉間ニ殺ス花ガ咲ク (旗)

緑陰に三人の老婆わらへりき (旗)

ピアノ鳴り, あなたに聖なる冬木と日 (旗)

切に濡らすวれより若き父母の墓 (変身)

ワルツやみ瓢箪光る黴の家 (今日)

春に飽き真黒き蝌蚪に飽き飽きす (今日)

海坂に日照るやここに孤絶の茸 (今日)

大寒の街に無数の拳ゆく (夜の桃)

夕焼へ群集だまり走り出す (夜の桃)

昇降機しづかに雷の夜を昇る (旗)

浮浪児のみな遠き眼に夏の船 (夜の桃)

一片の薔薇散る天地旱の中 (変身)

握りめし食う枯枝に帽子掛け (変身)

月の出の生々しさや湧き立つ蝗 (今日)

すみれ風一段高くボートの池 (変身)

鉄塊の疲れを白き蚊帳つつむ (今日)

松の花粉吸ひて先生胡桃割る (今日)

寒潮に雪降らす雲の上を飛ぶ (旗)

鏡餅暗きところに割れて坐す (変身)

みな大き袋を負へり雁渡る (夜の桃)

硬き土みつめて寒の牛あるく (変身)

機関銃眉間ニ殺ス花ガ咲ク (旗)

枝豆の真白き塩に愁眉ひらく (今日)

じわじわと西日金魚亡き水槽へ (変身)

松林の卓おむれつとわがひとり (旗)

兵隊がゆくまつ黒い汽車に乗り (旗)

春山を削りトロツコもて遊ぶ (今日)

雨の雲雀次ぎ次ぎわれを受渡す (今日)

天に鳴る春の烈風鶏よろめく (今日)

蚊の声の糸引く声が鉄壁へ (変身)

紅茸を怖れてわれを怖れずや (今日)

下駄はきて星を探しに雷後雨後 (変身)

露人ワシコフ叫びて石榴打ち落す (夜の桃)

秋耕のおのれの影を掘起す (夜の桃)

冬の園女の指を血つたひたり (旗)

空港に憲兵あゆむ寒き別離 (旗)

鯉幟王氏の窓に泳ぎ連れ (旗)

花冷えの城の石崖手で叩く(変身)

祝福を雨の雲雀に返上す (今日)

笑はざりしひと日の終り葡萄食ふ (旗)

夜の桜満ちて暗くて犬嚙合ふ (今日)

広島や卵食ふ時口をひらく (三鬼百句)

硝子の窓羽音たしかに露の鳥 (変身)

絶壁に寒き男女の顔ならぶ (旗)

貧農の軒とうもろこし石の硬さ (変身)

金銭に街の照り降り背に重し (旗)

僧を乗せしづかに黒い艦が出る (旗)

炎天の墓原独り子が通る (今日)

土用波へ腹の底より牛の声 (変身)

夕雲をつかみ歩きて蜘蛛定まる (変身)

虹の環に掘るや筋骨濡れ濡れて (変身)

荒園の力あつまり向日葵立つ (変身)

眼帯の内なる眼にも曼珠沙華 (変身)

胡坐居て熟柿を啜る心の喪 (夜の桃)

梅雨富士の黒い三角兄死ぬか (変身)

中年や独語おどろく夜の秋 (夜の桃)

西日中肩で押す貨車動き出す (今日)

愛撫する月下の犬に硬き骨 (変身)

馬と人泥田に挿さり労働祭 (変身)

高原の蝶噴き上げて草いきれ (変身)

野良犬よ落葉にうたれとび上がり (変身)

北風に重たき雄牛一歩一歩 (今日)

霜焼けの薔薇の蕾に飛行音 (変身)

崖下のかじかむ家に釘を打つ (今日)

びしよぬれの雪塊浮べ黒き河 (変身)

冬の山虹に踏まれて彫深し (今日)

寒の中コンクリートの中医師走る (変身)

雪山に雪降り友の妻も老ゆ (今日)

寒夜明け赤い造花が又も在る (変身)

悉く地べたに膝を抱けり捕虜 (旗)

青柿の下に悲しき事をいふ (夜の桃)

黒き月のせて三日月いつまで冬 (変身)

蕗を煮る男に鴉三声鳴く (夜の桃)

稲雀五重の塔を出発す (夜の桃)

働くや根のみの虹を地の上に (変身)

モナリザ常に硝子の中や冬つづく (今日)

不眠症魚は遠い海にゐる (旗)

十五夜の怒濤へ若き踊りの手 (変身)

つぎはぎの秋の国道乳房跳ね (変身)

黙契の雄牛と我を霰打つ (変身)

照る岩に刈麦干して山下る (変身)

満月下ブリキの家を打ち鳴らす (変身)

農婦来て秋のちまたに足強し (夜の桃)

秒針の強さよ凍る沼の岸 (夜の桃)

紅梅を去るや不幸に真向いて (夜の桃)

夏の闇火夫は火の色貨車通る (夜の桃)

夕焼けの牛の全身息はづむ (今日)

青柿は落つる外なし燈火なし (夜の桃)

傍観す女手に鏡餅割るを (変身)

禿山に飢ゑ砲弾を愛撫する (旗)

黒雲を雷が裂く夜のをんな達 (旗)

影のみがわが物炎天八方に (夜の桃)

百舌の声豆腐にひびくそれを切る (夜の桃)

竹伐り置く唐招提寺門前に (夜の桃)

しゆんぎくを播き水を飲みセロを弾く (夜の桃)

灯を消せば我が体のみ秋の闇 (夜の桃)

からかさを山の蜜柑がとんと打つ (夜の桃)

熱砂来て沖も左右も限りなし (夜の桃)

旱天やうつうつ通る青鴉 (夜の桃)

叫ぶ心百舌は梢に人は地に (夜の桃)

青年の大靴木の実地にめり込む (夜の桃)

眼中の蓮も揺れつつ夜帰る (夜の桃)

国飢ゑたりผわれも立ち見る冬の虹 (夜の桃)

大仏殿いでて桜にあたたまる (夜の桃)

愛撫する月下の犬に硬き骨 (変身)

春雷の下に氷塊来て並ぶ (夜の桃)

美しき寒夜の影を別ちけり (夜の桃)

甘藷を掘る一家の端にわれも掘る (今日)

電柱の上下寒し工夫登る (今日)

鉄道の大彎曲や横飛ぶ雪 (変身)

光る針縫いただよえり黴の家 (変身)

誕生日あかつきの雷顔の上に (旗)

旅毎日芙蓉が落ちし紅き音 (変身)

滑走輪冬山の天になほ廻る (旗)

厖大なる王氏の昼寝端午の日 (旗)

ゆるやかに確かに雲と麦伸びる (変身)

回る木馬一頭赤し春の昼 (変身)

電報の文字は「ユルセヨ」梅雨の星 (変身)

角砂糖前歯でかじる枯野の前 (変身)

屋上に草も木もなし病者と蝶 (今日)

電柱が今建ち春の雲集ふ (今日)

老年の口笛涼し青三日月 (夜の桃)

頭上げ下げ叫ぶ晩夏のぼろ鴉 (変身)

戦友ヲ葬リピストルヲ天ニ撃ツ (旗)

過去そのまま氷柱直下に突刺さる (今日)

火の玉の日が落つ凍る田を残し (今日)

冬の山虹に踏まれて彫深し (今日)

北風に重たき雄牛一歩一歩 (今日)

青梅が闇にびつしり泣く嬰児 (夜の桃)

眉と眼の間曇りて雪が降る (変身)

男・女良夜の水をとび越えし (夜の桃)

雪山に雪降り友の妻も老ゆ (今日)

杖上げて枯野の雲を縦に裂く (変身)

鯉幟王氏の窓に泳ぎ連れ (旗)

花冷えの城の石崖手で叩く (変身)

祝福を雨の雲雀に返上す (今日)

笑はざりしひと日の終り葡萄食ふ (旗)

夜の桜満ちて暗くて犬噛合ふ (今日)

広島や卵食ふ時口をひらく (三鬼百句)

硝子の窓羽音たしかに露の鳥 (変身)

絶壁に寒き男女の顔ならぶ (旗)

貧農の軒とうもろこし石の硬さ (変身)

金銭に街の照り降り背に重し (旗)

僧を乗せしづかに黒い艦が出る (旗)

炎天の墓原独り子が通る (今日)

土用波へ腹の底より牛の声 (変身)

夕雲をつかみ歩きて蜘蛛定まる (変身)

虹の環に掘るや筋骨濡れ濡れて (変身)

荒園の力あつまり向日葵立つ (変身)

眼帯の内なる眼にも曼珠沙華 (変身)

胡坐居て熟柿を啜る心の喪 (夜の桃)

梅雨富士の黒い三角兄死ぬか (変身)

中年や独語おどろく夜の秋 (夜の桃)

西日中肩で押す貨車動き出す (今日)

愛撫する月下の犬に硬き骨 (変身)

馬と人泥田に挿さり労働祭 (変身)

高原の蝶噴き上げて草いきれ (変身)

野良犬よ落葉にうたれとび上がり (変身)

北風に重たき雄牛一歩一歩 (今日)

霜焼けの薔薇の蕾に飛行音 (変身)

崖下のかじかむ家に釘を打つ (今日)

びしよぬれの雪塊浮べ黒き河 (変身)

冬の山虹に踏まれて彫深し (今日)

寒の中コンクリートの中医師走る (変身)

雪山に雪降り友の妻も老ゆ (今日)

寒夜明け赤い造花が又も在る (変身)

SANKI SAITŌ (1900-1962) was a Japanese poet and memorist, most famous for his modern haiku, which he began writing at thirty-three while practicing dentistry, and for which he was briefly imprisoned during the Second World War. His books include *Flags* (1940), *Night Peaches* (1948), *One Hundred Haiku* (1948), *Today* (1952), and *Transformations* (1962). "Sanki" is a nom de plume that means "Three Demons."

RYAN CHOI's first book was *In Dreams: The Very Short Stories of Ryunosuke Akutagawa*. He is an editor at *AGNI*. His writings and translations have appeared in *Harper's Magazine*, *Los Angeles Review of Books*, *The Nation*, *The New Criterion*, *Raritan*, *Times Literary Supplement*, and elsewhere. He lives in Honolulu, Hawaii, where he was born and raised.

9 781960 385277